Collecting good things to
Remember

Collecting good things to
Remember

Day ______________________________

Good stories that are collected

____

____

____

____

Day ______________________________

Good stories that are collected

____

____

____

____

Day ______________________________

Good stories that are collected

____

____

____

____

Collecting good things to
Remember

Day _______________________________

Good stories that are collected

____

____

____

____

Day _______________________________

Good stories that are collected

____

____

____

____

Day _______________________________

Good stories that are collected

____

____

____

____

Collecting good things to
Remember

Day _______________________________

Good stories that are collected

____
____
____
____

Day _______________________________

Good stories that are collected

____
____
____
____

Day _______________________________

Good stories that are collected

____
____
____
____

Collecting good things to
Remember

Day _______________________________

Good stories that are collected

____

____

____

____

Day _______________________________

Good stories that are collected

____

____

____

____

Day _______________________________

Good stories that are collected

____

____

____

____

Collecting good things to
Remember

Day _______________________

Good stories that are collected

____
____
____
____

Day _______________________

Good stories that are collected

____
____
____
____

Day _______________________

Good stories that are collected

____
____
____
____

Collecting good things to
Remember

Day _______________________________

Good stories that are collected

____

____

____

____

Day _______________________________

Good stories that are collected

____

____

____

____

Day _______________________________

Good stories that are collected

____

____

____

____

Collecting good things to
Remember

Day ___________________________

Good stories that are collected

____
____
____
____

Day ___________________________

Good stories that are collected

____
____
____
____

Day ___________________________

Good stories that are collected

____
____
____
____

Collecting good things to
Remember

Day _______________________

Good stories that are collected

____

____

____

____

Day _______________________

Good stories that are collected

____

____

____

____

Day _______________________

Good stories that are collected

____

____

____

____

Collecting good things to
Remember

Day _________________________________

Good stories that are collected

____
____
____

Day _________________________________

Good stories that are collected

____
____
____
____

Day _________________________________

Good stories that are collected

____
____
____
____

Collecting good things to
Remember

Day _______________________________

Good stories that are collected

____
____
____
____

Day _______________________________

Good stories that are collected

____
____
____
____

Day _______________________________

Good stories that are collected

____
____
____
____

Collecting good things to
Remember

Day ________________________

Good stories that are collected

____

____

____

____

Day ________________________

Good stories that are collected

____

____

____

____

Day ________________________

Good stories that are collected

____

____

____

____

Collecting good things to
Remember

Day _______________________________

Good stories that are collected

____
____
____
____

Day _______________________________

Good stories that are collected

____
____
____
____

Day _______________________________

Good stories that are collected

____
____
____
____

Collecting good things to
Remember

Day ___________________________

Good stories that are collected

____
____
____
____

Day ___________________________

Good stories that are collected

____
____
____
____

Day ___________________________

Good stories that are collected

____
____
____
____

Collecting good things to
Remember

Day _______________________________

Good stories that are collected

____
____
____
____

Day _______________________________

Good stories that are collected

____
____
____
____

Day _______________________________

Good stories that are collected

____
____
____
____

Collecting good things to
Remember

Day _______________________

Good stories that are collected

____
____
____
____

Day _______________________

Good stories that are collected

____
____
____
____

Day _______________________

Good stories that are collected

____
____
____
____

Collecting good things to
Remember

Day _______________________

Good stories that are collected

____
____
____
____

Day _______________________

Good stories that are collected

____
____
____
____

Day _______________________

Good stories that are collected

____
____
____
____

Collecting good things to
Remember

Day _________________________

Good stories that are collected

____

____

____

____

Day _________________________

Good stories that are collected

____

____

____

____

Day _________________________

Good stories that are collected

____

____

____

____

Collecting good things to
Remember

Day _______________________________

Good stories that are collected

____

____

____

____

Day _______________________________

Good stories that are collected

____

____

____

____

Day _______________________________

Good stories that are collected

____

____

____

____

Collecting good things to
Remember

Day ___________________________

Good stories that are collected

____
____
____
____

Day ___________________________

Good stories that are collected

____
____
____
____

Day ___________________________

Good stories that are collected

____
____
____
____

Collecting good things to
Remember

Day _______________________

Good stories that are collected

____
____
____

Day _______________________

Good stories that are collected

____
____
____

Day _______________________

Good stories that are collected

____
____
____

Collecting good things to
Remember

Day _______________________

Good stories that are collected

____
____
____
____

Day _______________________

Good stories that are collected

____
____
____
____

Day _______________________

Good stories that are collected

____
____
____
____

Collecting good things to
Remember

Day _______________________________

Good stories that are collected

____
____
____
____

Day _______________________________

Good stories that are collected

____
____
____
____

Day _______________________________

Good stories that are collected

____
____
____
____

Collecting good things to
Remember

Day _________________________

Good stories that are collected

____

____

____

____

Day _________________________

Good stories that are collected

____

____

____

____

Day _________________________

Good stories that are collected

____

____

____

____

Collecting good things to
Remember

Day _______________________

Good stories that are collected

____

____

____

Day _______________________

Good stories that are collected

____

____

____

Day _______________________

Good stories that are collected

____

____

____

Collecting good things to
Remember

Day _______________________________

Good stories that are collected

____

____

____

Day _______________________________

Good stories that are collected

____

____

____

Day _______________________________

Good stories that are collected

____

____

____

____

Collecting good things to
Remember

Day _____________________________

Good stories that are collected

____

____

____

____

Day _____________________________

Good stories that are collected

____

____

____

____

Day _____________________________

Good stories that are collected

____

____

____

____

Collecting good things to
Remember

Day _______________________________

Good stories that are collected

____

____

____

____

Day _______________________________

Good stories that are collected

____

____

____

____

Day _______________________________

Good stories that are collected

____

____

____

____

Collecting good things to
Remember

Day ___________________________

Good stories that are collected

____

____

____

____

Day ___________________________

Good stories that are collected

____

____

____

____

Day ___________________________

Good stories that are collected

____

____

____

____

Collecting good things to
Remember

Day _______________________________

Good stories that are collected

____

____

____

____

Day _______________________________

Good stories that are collected

____

____

____

____

Day _______________________________

Good stories that are collected

____

____

____

____

Collecting good things to
Remember

Day _______________________________

Good stories that are collected

____
____
____
____

Day _______________________________

Good stories that are collected

____
____
____
____

Day _______________________________

Good stories that are collected

____
____
____
____

Collecting good things to
Remember

Day _______________________

Good stories that are collected

____
____
____
____

Day _______________________

Good stories that are collected

____
____
____
____

Day _______________________

Good stories that are collected

____
____
____
____

Collecting good things to
Remember

Day _______________________

Good stories that are collected

____
____
____
____

Day _______________________

Good stories that are collected

____
____
____
____

Day _______________________

Good stories that are collected

____
____
____
____

Collecting good things to
Remember

Day _______________________

Good stories that are collected

____
____
____
____

Day _______________________

Good stories that are collected

____
____
____
____

Day _______________________

Good stories that are collected

____
____
____
____

Collecting good things to Remember

Day ___________________________

Good stories that are collected

____
____
____
____

Day ___________________________

Good stories that are collected

____
____
____
____

Day ___________________________

Good stories that are collected

____
____
____
____

Collecting good things to
Remember

Day ______________________________

Good stories that are collected

____

____

____

____

Day ______________________________

Good stories that are collected

____

____

____

____

Day ______________________________

Good stories that are collected

____

____

____

____

Collecting good things to
Remember

Day _______________________

Good stories that are collected

____
____
____
____

Day _______________________

Good stories that are collected

____
____
____
____

Day _______________________

Good stories that are collected

____
____
____
____

Collecting good things to
Remember

Day _______________________________

Good stories that are collected

____
____
____
____

Day _______________________________

Good stories that are collected

____
____
____
____

Day _______________________________

Good stories that are collected

____
____
____
____

Collecting good things to
Remember

Day ___________________________

Good stories that are collected

____

____

____

____

Day ___________________________

Good stories that are collected

____

____

____

____

Day ___________________________

Good stories that are collected

____

____

____

____

Collecting good things to
Remember

Day _______________________

Good stories that are collected

____
____
____
____

Day _______________________

Good stories that are collected

____
____
____
____

Day _______________________

Good stories that are collected

____
____
____
____

Collecting good things to
Remember

Day _______________________________

Good stories that are collected

____
____
____
____

Day _______________________________

Good stories that are collected

____
____
____
____

Day _______________________________

Good stories that are collected

____
____
____
____

Collecting good things to
Remember

Day _______________________________

Good stories that are collected

____

____

____

____

Day _______________________________

Good stories that are collected

____

____

____

____

Day _______________________________

Good stories that are collected

____

____

____

____

Collecting good things to
Remember

Day _______________________________

Good stories that are collected

____
____
____
____

Day _______________________________

Good stories that are collected

____
____
____
____

Day _______________________________

Good stories that are collected

____
____
____
____

Collecting good things to
Remember

Day ___________________________

Good stories that are collected

____

____

____

____

Day ___________________________

Good stories that are collected

____

____

____

____

Day ___________________________

Good stories that are collected

____

____

____

____

Collecting good things to
Remember

Day _______________________________

Good stories that are collected

____
____
____
____

Day _______________________________

Good stories that are collected

____
____
____
____

Day _______________________________

Good stories that are collected

____
____
____
____

Collecting good things to
Remember

Day _______________________________

Good stories that are collected

____
____
____
____

Day _______________________________

Good stories that are collected

____
____
____
____

Day _______________________________

Good stories that are collected

____
____
____
____

Collecting good things to
Remember

Day _______________________________

Good stories that are collected

____

____

____

____

Day _______________________________

Good stories that are collected

____

____

____

____

Day _______________________________

Good stories that are collected

____

____

____

____

Collecting good things to
Remember

Day _______________________________

Good stories that are collected

____
____
____
____

Day _______________________________

Good stories that are collected

____
____
____
____

Day _______________________________

Good stories that are collected

____
____
____
____

Collecting good things to
Remember

Day _______________________________

Good stories that are collected

____

____

____

____

Day _______________________________

Good stories that are collected

____

____

____

____

Day _______________________________

Good stories that are collected

____

____

____

____

Collecting good things to
Remember

Day _______________________

Good stories that are collected

____
____
____
____

Day _______________________

Good stories that are collected

____
____
____
____

Day _______________________

Good stories that are collected

____
____
____
____

Collecting good things to
Remember

Day ________________________

Good stories that are collected

____

____

____

____

Day ________________________

Good stories that are collected

____

____

____

____

Day ________________________

Good stories that are collected

____

____

____

____

Collecting good things to
Remember

Day _______________________

Good stories that are collected

____
____
____
____

Day _______________________

Good stories that are collected

____
____
____
____

Day _______________________

Good stories that are collected

____
____
____
____

Collecting good things to
Remember

Day _______________________________

Good stories that are collected

____

____

____

____

Day _______________________________

Good stories that are collected

____

____

____

____

Day _______________________________

Good stories that are collected

____

____

____

____

Collecting good things to
Remember

Day _______________________

Good stories that are collected

____
____
____
____

Day _______________________

Good stories that are collected

____
____
____
____

Day _______________________

Good stories that are collected

____
____
____
____

Collecting good things to
Remember

Day _______________________________

Good stories that are collected

____

____

____

____

Day _______________________________

Good stories that are collected

____

____

____

____

Day _______________________________

Good stories that are collected

____

____

____

____

Collecting good things to
Remember

Day _______________________________

Good stories that are collected

____
____
____
____

Day _______________________________

Good stories that are collected

____
____
____
____

Day _______________________________

Good stories that are collected

____
____
____
____

Collecting good things to
Remember

Day _______________________________

Good stories that are collected

____
____
____
____

Day _______________________________

Good stories that are collected

____
____
____
____

Day _______________________________

Good stories that are collected

____
____
____
____

Collecting good things to
Remember

Day _______________________

Good stories that are collected

____

____

____

____

Day _______________________

Good stories that are collected

____

____

____

____

Day _______________________

Good stories that are collected

____

____

____

____

Collecting good things to
Remember

Day _______________________________

Good stories that are collected

____
____
____
____

Day _______________________________

Good stories that are collected

____
____
____
____

Day _______________________________

Good stories that are collected

____
____
____
____

Collecting good things to
Remember

Day _______________________________

Good stories that are collected

____
____
____

Day _______________________________

Good stories that are collected

____
____
____

Day _______________________________

Good stories that are collected

____
____
____

Collecting good things to
Remember

Day ___________________________

Good stories that are collected

____
____
____
____

Day ___________________________

Good stories that are collected

____
____
____
____

Day ___________________________

Good stories that are collected

____
____
____
____

Collecting good things to
Remember

Day _______________________________

Good stories that are collected

____
____
____
____

Day _______________________________

Good stories that are collected

____
____
____
____

Day _______________________________

Good stories that are collected

____
____
____
____

Collecting good things to
Remember

Day _______________________________

Good stories that are collected

____
____
____
____

Day _______________________________

Good stories that are collected

____
____
____
____

Day _______________________________

Good stories that are collected

____
____
____

Collecting good things to
Remember

Day _______________________________

Good stories that are collected

____

____

____

Day _______________________________

Good stories that are collected

____

____

____

Day _______________________________

Good stories that are collected

____

____

____

Collecting good things to
Remember

Day ___________________________

Good stories that are collected

____

____

____

____

Day ___________________________

Good stories that are collected

____

____

____

____

Day ___________________________

Good stories that are collected

____

____

____

____

Collecting good things to
Remember

Day _______________________________

Good stories that are collected

____

____

____

____

Day _______________________________

Good stories that are collected

____

____

____

____

Day _______________________________

Good stories that are collected

____

____

____

____

Collecting good things to
Remember

Day _______________________

Good stories that are collected

____
____
____
____

Day _______________________

Good stories that are collected

____
____
____
____

Day _______________________

Good stories that are collected

____
____
____
____

Collecting good things to
Remember

Day _______________________

Good stories that are collected

____
____
____
____

Day _______________________

Good stories that are collected

____
____
____
____

Day _______________________

Good stories that are collected

____
____
____
____

Collecting good things to
Remember

Day _______________________

Good stories that are collected

____

____

____

Day _______________________

Good stories that are collected

____

____

____

Day _______________________

Good stories that are collected

____

____

____

Collecting good things to
Remember

Day _______________________________

Good stories that are collected

____
____
____

Day _______________________________

Good stories that are collected

____
____
____

Day _______________________________

Good stories that are collected

____
____
____

Collecting good things to
Remember

Day ___________________________

Good stories that are collected

____
____
____
____

Day ___________________________

Good stories that are collected

____
____
____
____

Day ___________________________

Good stories that are collected

____
____
____
____

Collecting good things to
Remember

Day _______________________________

Good stories that are collected

____

____

____

____

Day _______________________________

Good stories that are collected

____

____

____

____

Day _______________________________

Good stories that are collected

____

____

____

____

Collecting good things to
Remember

Day _______________________________

Good stories that are collected

____

____

____

____

Day _______________________________

Good stories that are collected

____

____

____

____

Day _______________________________

Good stories that are collected

____

____

____

____

Collecting good things to
Remember

Day ___________________________

Good stories that are collected

____
____
____
____

Day ___________________________

Good stories that are collected

____
____
____
____

Day ___________________________

Good stories that are collected

____
____
____
____

Collecting good things to
Remember

Day _______________________

Good stories that are collected

____

____

____

____

Day _______________________

Good stories that are collected

____

____

____

____

Day _______________________

Good stories that are collected

____

____

____

____

Collecting good things to
Remember

Day ___________________________

Good stories that are collected

____

____

____

____

Day ___________________________

Good stories that are collected

____

____

____

____

Day ___________________________

Good stories that are collected

____

____

____

____

Collecting good things to
Remember

Day _______________________________

Good stories that are collected

____
____
____
____

Day _______________________________

Good stories that are collected

____
____
____
____

Day _______________________________

Good stories that are collected

____
____
____
____

Collecting good things to
Remember

Day _______________________

Good stories that are collected

____
____
____
____

Day _______________________

Good stories that are collected

____
____
____
____

Day _______________________

Good stories that are collected

____
____
____
____

Collecting good things to
Remember

Day _______________________________

Good stories that are collected

____

____

____

Day _______________________________

Good stories that are collected

____

____

____

____

Day _______________________________

Good stories that are collected

____

____

____

____

Collecting good things to
Remember

Day ___________________________

Good stories that are collected

____

____

____

____

Day ___________________________

Good stories that are collected

____

____

____

____

Day ___________________________

Good stories that are collected

____

____

____

____

Collecting good things to Remember

Day _______________________________

Good stories that are collected

____
____
____
____

Day _______________________________

Good stories that are collected

____
____
____
____

Day _______________________________

Good stories that are collected

____
____
____
____

Collecting good things to
Remember

Day ___________________________

Good stories that are collected

____
____
____
____

Day ___________________________

Good stories that are collected

____
____
____
____

Day ___________________________

Good stories that are collected

____
____
____
____

Collecting good things to
Remember

Day ___________________________

Good stories that are collected

____
____
____
____

Day ___________________________

Good stories that are collected

____
____
____
____

Day ___________________________

Good stories that are collected

____
____
____
____

Collecting good things to
Remember

Day ___________________________

Good stories that are collected

____

____

____

____

Day ___________________________

Good stories that are collected

____

____

____

____

Day ___________________________

Good stories that are collected

____

____

____

____

Collecting good things to
Remember

Day _______________________

Good stories that are collected

____

____

____

____

Day _______________________

Good stories that are collected

____

____

____

____

Day _______________________

Good stories that are collected

____

____

____

____

Collecting good things to
Remember

Day _______________________

Good stories that are collected

____
____
____
____

Day _______________________

Good stories that are collected

____
____
____
____

Day _______________________

Good stories that are collected

____
____
____
____

Collecting good things to
Remember

Day _______________________________

Good stories that are collected

____
____
____
____

Day _______________________________

Good stories that are collected

____
____
____
____

Day _______________________________

Good stories that are collected

____
____
____
____

Collecting good things to
Remember

Day _______________________

Good stories that are collected

____
____
____
____

Day _______________________

Good stories that are collected

____
____
____
____

Day _______________________

Good stories that are collected

____
____
____
____

Collecting good things to
Remember

Day _______________________

Good stories that are collected

____

____

____

____

Day _______________________

Good stories that are collected

____

____

____

____

Day _______________________

Good stories that are collected

____

____

____

____

Collecting good things to
Remember

Day _______________________________

Good stories that are collected

____

____

____

____

Day _______________________________

Good stories that are collected

____

____

____

____

Day _______________________________

Good stories that are collected

____

____

____

____

Collecting good things to
Remember

Day _______________________________

Good stories that are collected

____
____
____
____

Day _______________________________

Good stories that are collected

____
____
____
____

Day _______________________________

Good stories that are collected

____
____
____

Collecting good things to
Remember

Day ________________________________

Good stories that are collected

____

____

____

____

Day ________________________________

Good stories that are collected

____

____

____

____

Day ________________________________

Good stories that are collected

____

____

____

____

Collecting good things to
Remember

Day _______________________________

Good stories that are collected

____

____

____

____

Day _______________________________

Good stories that are collected

____

____

____

____

Day _______________________________

Good stories that are collected

____

____

____

____

Collecting good things to
Remember

Day _______________________________

Good stories that are collected

____

____

____

____

Day _______________________________

Good stories that are collected

____

____

____

____

Day _______________________________

Good stories that are collected

____

____

____

____

Collecting good things to
Remember

Day _______________________________

Good stories that are collected

____
____
____
____

Day _______________________________

Good stories that are collected

____
____
____
____

Day _______________________________

Good stories that are collected

____
____
____
____

Collecting good things to
Remember

Day _______________________________

Good stories that are collected

____

____

____

____

Day _______________________________

Good stories that are collected

____

____

____

____

Day _______________________________

Good stories that are collected

____

____

____

____

Collecting good things to
Remember

Day ___________________________

Good stories that are collected

____

____

____

____

Day ___________________________

Good stories that are collected

____

____

____

____

Day ___________________________

Good stories that are collected

____

____

____

____

Collecting good things to
Remember

Day ________________________

Good stories that are collected

____

____

____

____

Day ________________________

Good stories that are collected

____

____

____

____

Day ________________________

Good stories that are collected

____

____

____

____

Collecting good things to
Remember

Day _______________________

Good stories that are collected

____
____
____
____

Day _______________________

Good stories that are collected

____
____
____
____

Day _______________________

Good stories that are collected

____
____
____
____

Collecting good things to
Remember

Day _______________________

Good stories that are collected

____
____
____
____

Day _______________________

Good stories that are collected

____
____
____
____

Day _______________________

Good stories that are collected

____
____
____
____

Collecting good things to
Remember

Day ___________________________

Good stories that are collected

____
____
____
____

Day ___________________________

Good stories that are collected

____
____
____
____

Day ___________________________

Good stories that are collected

____
____
____
____

Collecting good things to
Remember

Day _______________________________

Good stories that are collected

____

____

____

____

Day _______________________________

Good stories that are collected

____

____

____

____

Day _______________________________

Good stories that are collected

____

____

____

____

Collecting good things to
Remember

Day _______________________

Good stories that are collected

____
____
____
____

Day _______________________

Good stories that are collected

____
____
____
____

Day _______________________

Good stories that are collected

____
____
____
____

Collecting good things to
Remember

Day _______________________

Good stories that are collected

____
____
____
____

Day _______________________

Good stories that are collected

____
____
____
____

Day _______________________

Good stories that are collected

____
____
____
____

Collecting good things to
Remember

Day _______________________________

Good stories that are collected

____

____

____

____

Day _______________________________

Good stories that are collected

____

____

____

____

Day _______________________________

Good stories that are collected

____

____

____

____

Collecting good things to
Remember

Day _______________________

Good stories that are collected

____
____
____
____

Day _______________________

Good stories that are collected

____
____
____
____

Day _______________________

Good stories that are collected

____
____
____
____

Collecting good things to
Remember

Day ______________________________

Good stories that are collected

____

____

____

____

Day ______________________________

Good stories that are collected

____

____

____

____

Day ______________________________

Good stories that are collected

____

____

____

____

Collecting good things to
Remember

Day _______________________________

Good stories that are collected

____
____
____
____

Day _______________________________

Good stories that are collected

____
____
____
____

Day _______________________________

Good stories that are collected

____
____
____
____

Collecting good things to
Remember

Day ________________________________

Good stories that are collected

____

____

____

____

Day ________________________________

Good stories that are collected

____

____

____

____

Day ________________________________

Good stories that are collected

____

____

____

____

Collecting good things to
Remember

Day _______________________

Good stories that are collected

____
____
____
____

Day _______________________

Good stories that are collected

____
____
____
____

Day _______________________

Good stories that are collected

____
____
____
____

Collecting good things to
Remember

Day _______________________________

Good stories that are collected

____

____

____

____

Day _______________________________

Good stories that are collected

____

____

____

____

Day _______________________________

Good stories that are collected

____

____

____

____

Collecting good things to
Remember

Day ________________________________

Good stories that are collected

____
____
____
____

Day ________________________________

Good stories that are collected

____
____
____
____

Day ________________________________

Good stories that are collected

____
____
____
____

Collecting good things to
Remember

Day _______________________________

Good stories that are collected

____
____
____
____

Day _______________________________

Good stories that are collected

____
____
____
____

Day _______________________________

Good stories that are collected

____
____
____
____

Collecting good things to
Remember

Day _______________________________

Good stories that are collected

____

____

____

____

Day _______________________________

Good stories that are collected

____

____

____

____

Day _______________________________

Good stories that are collected

____

____

____

____

Collecting good things to
Remember

Day _______________________________

Good stories that are collected

____
____
____
____

Day _______________________________

Good stories that are collected

____
____
____
____

Day _______________________________

Good stories that are collected

____
____
____
____

Collecting good things to
Remember

Day _______________________________

Good stories that are collected

____
____
____
____

Day _______________________________

Good stories that are collected

____
____
____
____

Day _______________________________

Good stories that are collected

____
____
____
____

Collecting good things to
Remember

Day _______________________

Good stories that are collected

____
____
____
____

Day _______________________

Good stories that are collected

____
____
____
____

Day _______________________

Good stories that are collected

____
____
____
____

Collecting good things to
Remember

Day ___________________________

Good stories that are collected

____
____
____

Day ___________________________

Good stories that are collected

____
____
____

Day ___________________________

Good stories that are collected

____
____
____
____

Collecting good things to
Remember

Day ___________________________

Good stories that are collected

____

____

____

____

Day ___________________________

Good stories that are collected

____

____

____

____

Day ___________________________

Good stories that are collected

____

____

____

____

Collecting good things to
Remember

Day _______________________________

Good stories that are collected

____
____
____
____

Day _______________________________

Good stories that are collected

____
____
____
____

Day _______________________________

Good stories that are collected

____
____
____
____

Collecting good things to
Remember

Day _______________________________

Good stories that are collected

____
____
____
____

Day _______________________________

Good stories that are collected

____
____
____
____

Day _______________________________

Good stories that are collected

____
____
____
____

Collecting good things to
Remember

Day _______________________________

Good stories that are collected

____
____
____
____

Day _______________________________

Good stories that are collected

____
____
____
____

Day _______________________________

Good stories that are collected

____
____
____
____

Collecting good things to
Remember

Day _______________________________

Good stories that are collected

____
____
____
____

Day _______________________________

Good stories that are collected

____
____
____
____

Day _______________________________

Good stories that are collected

____
____
____
____